MW00963745

Level C

LANGUAGE Exercises

TEACHER'S GUIDE

Betty Jones
Saranna Moeller
Cynthia T. Strauch

STECK-VAUGHN
ELEMENTARY · SECONDARY · ADULT · LIBRARY

A Harcourt Company

www.steck-vaughn.com

Table of Contents

Acknowledgments

Executive Editor: Diane Sharpe
Supervising Editor: Stephanie Muller
Project Editor: Patricia Claney
Design Manager: Laura Cole

LANGUAGE EXERCISES Series:

Level A	Level D	Level G
Level B	Level E	Level H
Level C	Level F	Review

ISBN 0-8114-6316-8

6 7 8 9 0 RP 00

Language Exercises is a program designed for students who require additional practice in the basics of effective writing and speaking. Focused practice in key grammar, usage, mechanics, and composition areas helps students gain ownership of essential skills. The logical sequence of the practice exercises, combined with a clear and concise format, allows for easy and independent use.

Focus on Key Skills

Language Exercises provides systematic, focused attention to just one carefully selected skill at a time. Rules are clearly stated at the beginning of each lesson. Key terms are introduced in bold type. The rules are then illustrated with examples and followed by meaningful practice exercises.

Lessons are organized around a series of units. They are arranged in a logical sequence beginning with vocabulary, progressing through sentences, grammar and usage, mechanics, and culminating with composition skills.

Levels C through H and Review include a final unit on study skills, which can be assigned as needed. This unit includes such skills as organizing information, following directions, using a dictionary, using the library, and choosing appropriate reference sources.

Skills are reviewed thoroughly in a two-page Review at the conclusion of each unit and in the twelve-page Final Review at the end of the book. Also, the last twelve pages of this Teacher's Guide provide six two-page blackline master Unit Tests presented in a standardized test format. The content of each unit is repeated and expanded in subsequent levels as highlighted in the Scope and Sequence chart on the next two pages.

Application Is the Key

Throughout the program, *Language Exercises* stresses the application of language principles. In addition to matching, circling, or underlining elements in a predetermined sentence, lessons ask students to use what they have learned in an original sentence or in rewriting a sentence. *Using What You've Learned,* a two-page lesson at the end of each unit, provides students with an opportunity to "pull together" what they have learned in the unit and apply their learning to a writing situation.

Easy-to-Use Lessons

From the beginning, students feel comfortable with the format of the lessons. Each lesson is introduced with a rule at the top of the page and ends with a meaningful exercise at the bottom of the page. Each lesson is clearly labeled, and directions are clear and uncomplicated. Because the format is logical and consistent and the vocabulary is carefully controlled, most students can use *Language Exercises* with a high degree of independence. As the teacher, this allows you the time needed to help students on a one-to-one basis.

Attention to Composition Skills

The process approach to teaching writing provides success for most students. *Language Exercises* provides direct support for the teaching of composition and significantly enhances those strategies and techniques commonly associated with the process-writing approach.

Each book includes a composition unit that provides substantial work with important composition skills, such as writing topic sentences, selecting supporting details, taking notes, writing reports, and revising and proofreading. Also included in the composition unit is practice with various prewriting activities, such as clustering and brainstorming, which play an important role in process writing. The composition lessons are presented in the same rule-plus-practice format as in other units.

Teacher's Guide

The Teacher's Guide for each level of *Language Exercises* includes a two-page Scope and Sequence chart and an Answer Key in an easy-to-use format for all exercises.

The final section of the Teacher's Guide includes six two-page blackline master Unit Tests presented in a standardized test format. The skills and concepts included on these tests parallel the skills in the end-of-unit Reviews in the student book. These Unit Tests can also be used as both pre- and post-tests. Answers for these tests appear at the end of the Answer Key.

SCOPE AND SEQUENCE

	A	B	C	D	E	F	G	H	Review
Vocabulary									
Sound Words (Onomatopoeia)	■								
Rhyming Words	■	■							
Synonyms	■	■	■	■	■	■	■	■	■
Antonyms	■	■	■	■	■	■	■	■	■
Homonyms	■	■	■	■	■	■	■	■	■
Multiple Meanings/Homographs	■	■	■	■	■	■	■	■	■
Prefixes and Suffixes			■	■	■	■	■	■	■
Base and Root Words			■	■	■	■	■	■	■
Compound Words			■	■	■	■	■	■	■
Contractions			■	■	■	■	■	■	■
Idioms						■	■	■	■
Connotation/Denotation						■	■	■	■
Sentences									
Word Order in Sentences	■	■							
Recognizing a Sentence	■	■	■	■	■	■	■	■	■
Subjects and Predicates	■	■	■	■	■	■	■	■	■
Types of Sentences	■	■	■	■	■	■	■	■	■
Compound/Complex Sentences			■	■	■	■	■	■	■
Sentence Combining			■	■	■	■	■	■	■
Run-On Sentences			■	■	■	■	■	■	■
Independent and Subordinate Clauses							■	■	■
Compound Subjects and Predicates						■	■	■	■
Direct and Indirect Objects							■	■	■
Inverted Word Order						■	■	■	■
Grammar and Usage									
Common and Proper Nouns	■	■	■	■	■	■	■	■	■
Singular and Plural Nouns	■	■	■	■	■	■	■	■	■
Possessive Nouns			■	■	■	■	■	■	■
Appositives						■	■	■	■
Verbs	■	■	■	■	■	■	■	■	■
Verb Tense	■	■	■	■	■	■	■	■	■
Regular/Irregular Verbs	■	■	■	■	■	■	■	■	■
Subject/Verb Agreement			■	■	■	■	■	■	■
Verb Phrases						■	■	■	■
Transitive and Intransitive Verbs							■	■	■
Verbals: Gerunds, Participles, and Infinitives							■	■	■
Active and Passive Voice							■	■	■
Mood								■	■
Pronouns	■	■	■	■	■	■	■	■	■
Antecedents							■	■	■
Articles	■	■	■						
Adjectives	■	■	■	■	■	■	■	■	■
Correct Word Usage (e.g. *may/can, sit/set*)	■	■	■	■	■	■	■	■	■
Adverbs			■	■	■	■	■	■	■
Prepositions				■	■	■	■	■	■
Prepositional Phrases						■	■	■	■
Conjunctions						■	■	■	■
Interjections						■	■	■	
Double Negatives								■	■
Capitalization and Punctuation									
Capitalization: First Word in Sentence	■	■	■	■	■	■	■		■
Capitalization: Proper Nouns	■	■	■	■	■	■	■	■	■
Capitalization: in Letters			■	■	■	■	■	■	■
Capitalization: Abbreviations			■	■	■	■	■	■	■
Capitalization: Titles		■	■	■	■	■	■	■	■

	A	B	C	D	E	F	G	H	Review
Capitalization and Punctuation (cont'd)									
Capitalization: Proper Adjectives					■	■	■	■	■
End Punctuation	■	■	■	■	■	■	■	■	■
Commas		■	■	■	■	■	■	■	■
Apostrophes in Contractions		■	■	■	■	■	■	■	■
Apostrophes in Possessives			■	■	■	■	■	■	■
Quotation Marks			■	■	■	■	■	■	■
Colons/Semicolons						■	■	■	■
Hyphens						■	■	■	■
Composition									
Expanding Sentences					■	■	■	■	■
Writing a Paragraph		■	■	■	■	■	■	■	■
Paragraphs: Topic Sentence (main idea)		■	■	■	■	■	■	■	■
Paragraphs: Supporting Details		■	■	■	■	■	■	■	■
Order In Paragraphs		■	■	■	■	■	■		■
Writing Process:									
Establishing Purpose			■	■		■	■	■	■
Audience					■	■	■	■	■
Topic			■	■	■	■	■		
Outlining				■		■	■	■	■
Clustering/Brainstorming					■		■	■	■
Notetaking						■	■		
Revising/Proofreading					■	■	■	■	■
Types of Writing:									
Poem	■								
Letter	■	■	■			■			
"How-to" Paragraph				■					
Invitation				■					
Telephone Message				■					
Conversation				■					
Narrative Paragraph				■					
Comparing and Contrasting					■				
Descriptive Paragraph					■				
Report						■			
Interview							■		
Persuasive Composition								■	■
Readiness/Study Skills									
Grouping	■								
Letters of Alphabet	■								
Listening	■	■							
Making Comparisons	■	■							
Organizing Information	■	■	■						
Following Directions	■	■	■	■	■				
Alphabetical Order	■	■	■	■	■	■	■	■	■
Using a Dictionary:									
Definitions		■	■	■	■	■	■	■	■
Guide Words/Entry Words		■	■	■	■	■	■	■	■
Syllables			■	■	■	■	■	■	■
Pronunciation			■	■	■	■	■	■	■
Multiple Meanings				■	■	■	■	■	■
Word Origins						■	■	■	■
Parts of a Book			■	■	■	■	■	■	■
Using the Library						■	■		■
Using Encyclopedias				■	■	■	■		■
Using Reference Books						■	■		■
Using the *Readers' Guide*						■	■		■
Using Tables, Charts, Graphs, and Diagrams						■	■	■	■
Choosing Appropriate Sources						■	■		■

Unit 1 Vocabulary

Lesson 1, Synonyms (P. 1)

Top:

Many people have heard <u>stories</u> about the Cyclops. He was a <u>huge</u> monster. He had a <u>body</u> like a <u>person</u>. But his face was <u>unusual</u>. He had only one eye in the <u>middle</u> of his forehead. <u>His</u> <u>home</u> was a cave on an island. <u>The</u> people who lived near <u>the</u> island were <u>afraid</u> of the Cyclops. He was very mean and <u>noisy</u>.

Bottom:
Sentences will vary.

Lesson 2, Antonyms (P. 2)

Top:

A gerbil is a <u>small</u>, furry animal. It has long <u>back</u> legs. Its tail is <u>long</u> and <u>hairy</u>. A gerbil is <u>easy</u> to care for, and it is a fun pet. It loves to <u>play</u>.

Bottom:
1. Do you think Ann will win or lose?
2. Will he do a backbend now or later?

Lesson 3, Homonyms (P. 3)

Top:
1. their
2. there
3. they're
4. their
5. there
6. they're
7. their

Bottom:
Sentences will vary.

Lesson 4, More Homonyms (P. 4)

Top:
1. here
2. to
3. hear
4. two
5. too
6. hear
7. to
8. Here
9. two
10. hear

Bottom:
Sentences will vary.

Lesson 5, Words with More Than One Meaning (P. 5)

Top:
1. 2
2. 2
3. 1
4. 2
5. 1
6. 1
7. 1
8. 2

Bottom:
Sentences will vary.

Lesson 6, Prefixes (P. 6)

Top:
1. unhappy, not happy
2. unfair, not fair
3. uneven, not even
4. unsafe, not safe
5. untie, not tied or the opposite of tie

Middle:
1. reopen, open again
2. retest, test again
3. reuse, use again
4. reread, read again

Bottom:
Sentences will vary.

Lesson 7, Suffixes (P. 7)

Top:
1. climber
2. teacher
3. visitor
4. traveler
5. actor
6. marker
7. painter
8. singer

Bottom:
1. The gardener clipped the roses.
2. He cleaned his gloves in the washer.
3. He and the farmer ate lunch.
4. Then he hired a new worker to help him.
5. The new worker used to be a teacher.

Lesson 8, Compound Words (P. 8)

Top:
1. birthday
2. afternoon
3. skateboard
4. fireplace
5. catfish

6. rainbow
7. snowball
8. sunrise
9. waterfall
10. downstairs

Bottom:
1. birth   day
2. every   one
3. down   stairs
4. Every   thing
5. class   mate
6. foot   ball

Lesson 9, Contractions (P. 9)

Top:
1. She's going camping this weekend.
2. I think she'll go fishing in the lake.
3. Inuk doesn't like to fish.
4. Here's some fresh bait.
5. There's enough for everyone to use.
6. After we catch the fish, I'll help cook them.
7. It isn't hard to do.

Bottom:
Sentences will vary.

Review (P. 10)

1. tiny
2. easy
3. leap
4. rear
5. enjoys

1. last
2. sad
3. small
4. wide
5. slow

1. here
2. to
3. two
4. They're
5. their
6. too
7. hear

Review (P. 11)

1. Sentences will vary.
2. Sentences will vary.

1. Sentences will vary.
2. Sentences will vary.

1. unpack
2. recopy
3. untie
4. relive
5. remake

6. retake
7. rename
8. untrue
9. unsure

1. cleaner
2. visitor
3. worker
4. teacher
5. dryer
6. actor
7. heater
8. leader
9. sailor

Students should circle the words in bold.
1. There's the **tightrope**.
2. We'll be **inside** the tent.
3. The clown isn't in the **airplane**.
4. We can't see **everything**.
5. Let's eat **something**.
6. Doesn't **everyone** like the circus?

Using What You've Learned (P. 12)

Dear Tom,
    It was very hot here in the house today. I went to the pool to cool off. My two friends, Anna and Rosa, were there. We didn't do anything but swim. We'll go back tomorrow. I hear it'll be even hotter then. I'll be sure to tell Anna and Rosa to bring their beach ball.

Using What You've Learned (P. 13)

Stories will vary.

 **Unit 2**   Sentences

Lesson 10, Sentences (P. 14)

Top:
1, 3, 5, and 7 are sentences.

Bottom:
1. The ants marched in a row.
2. They were looking for crumbs.
3. Eva saw them coming.
4. She moved her blanket right away.
5. The food was for Eva, not the ants.

Lesson 11, Identifying Sentences (P. 15)

Top:
1. Catherine saw Superdog.
2. Superdog flew high.
3. Where is Superdog?
4. Superdog read about the dog show.

5. Superdog went to the show.
6. Did he win a blue ribbon?
7. Superdog won "Best of Show."

Bottom:
Students should draw a line through the following:
Surprised all the judges.
The judges in the chairs.
Jumped over a tall building in a single bound.

Lesson 12, Statements and Questions (P. 16)

Top:
1. S
2. Q
3. S
4. S
5. Q
6. S
7. S
8. S
9. Q
10. Q

Bottom:
Many people visit Hawaii to ride the waves. Which beach do they like best?

Lesson 13, Commands and Exclamations (P. 17)

Top:
1. E
2. C
3. C
4. E
5. C
6. E
7. C
8. E
9. E

Bottom:
Sentences will vary.

Lesson 14, Subjects in Sentences (P. 18)

Top:
1. We went sledding today.
2. The sled flew down the hill.
3. Jamie threw a snowball.
4. Kamal lost his hat.
5. Skaters were on the pond.
6. The ice was smooth.
7. Alan liked to spin around.
8. He went very fast.
9. The girls slid by us.
10. A red glove was in the snow.

Bottom:
Sentences will vary.

Lesson 15, Predicates in Sentences (P. 19)

Top:
1. The cub growled at the bird.
2. The huge ape swung from a bar.
3. Barry liked the camels.
4. These tiny snakes are harmless.
5. Monkeys are fun to watch.
6. Vic petted the sheep.
7. A calf was in the yard.
8. Lee saw the baby ducks.
9. The pigs cooled off.
10. An owl hooted softly.

Bottom:
Sentences will vary.

Lesson 16, Combining Subjects and Predicates (P. 20)

1. Mom and Trish went on the ride.
2. Bob and the boys stood in line.
3. Lee and Jung ate lunch.
4. Donna took a picture and sat down to rest.
5. Ed popped the balloons and won a prize.
6. Linda went to the petting zoo and fed the animals.
7. Ryan saw the bears and rode on the train.

Lesson 17, Combining Sentences (P. 21)

Top:
1. The wind howled, and the sand blew around.
2. The children can swim, or they can play ball.
3. The water is cold, but the sand is warm.
4. The sea is blue, and the foam is white.
5. Dad carried our lunch, and we carried the chairs.

Bottom:
1. Take your pail, and fill it with sand.
2. You can make a castle, or you can make a cave.
3. We can't play on rocks, but we can play on sand.

Lesson 18, Writing Clear Sentences (P. 22)

1. The seeds must be planted.
   This is done in many ways.
2. A seed floated in the breeze.
   It was very windy.
3. You can eat these seeds.
   Shameka will gather some more.
4. Birds and animals eat seeds.
   You can buy seeds for them in a store.

Review (P. 23)

1. Owls have large eyes.
2. They live in the ocean.
3. Lizards are reptiles.
4. Do you like chipmunks?

1. Q
2. S
3. Q
4. S

1. C
2. E
3. C
4. E

Students should circle the words in bold.
1. The cat **washed its face with its paw**.
2. Kirk **threw a ball of yarn to the cat**.
3. The cat **took a long nap**.
4. Kirk **fed the cat after its nap**.

Review (P. 24)

1. Erin fed her mouse and cleaned its cage.
2. Raul and Ann held the mouse.
3. The mouse feels warm, but its nose feels cool.

1. My friend comes over. My dad takes us to see a movie.
2. We stand in line. We get our tickets.
3. We find a place to sit. We share some popcorn.
4. The theater gets dark. The movie begins.

Using What You've Learned (P. 25)

The sea horse is an amazing animal! It is only about five inches tall and is covered with bony plates. The sea horse swims by using the fin on its back, but it is not a strong swimmer. Ocean currents carry it and move the sea horse from one place to another. The sea horse can easily stop itself. It just wraps its tail around a sea plant.

Using What You've Learned (P. 26)

Stories will vary.

 ## Unit 3 Grammar and Usage

Lesson 19, Nouns (P. 27)

Top:
1. The astronaut looked out the window.
2. Clouds circled the earth.
3. The ocean looked like a lake.
4. Another astronaut ate her lunch.
5. An apple floated inside the cabin.
6. One man put on his spacesuit.
7. The astronaut walked in space.
8. The newspaper had pictures of him.

Bottom:
1. ocean
2. ship
3. doctor
4. radio
5. cheer
6. day

Lesson 20, Singular and Plural Nouns (P. 28)

Top:
1. skates
2. cars
3. parades
4. toes
5. brushes
6. classes
7. inches
8. boxes
9. dishes
10. dollars
11. leashes
12. watches

Bottom:
1. The fish are in a new tank.
2. All the plants are fresh.
3. Use that net to catch the fish.
4. Both those boys visit the fish store.

Lesson 21, Common and Proper Nouns (P. 29)

Top:
1. C   7. C
2. P   8. P
3. C   9. P
4. C   10. P
5. P   11. C
6. P   12. C

Bottom:
Students should circle the words in bold.
1. The ocean was very rough on **Tuesday**.
2. The waves pounded **Sand Beach**.
3. The beach is in **Mexico**.
4. Some boys were there from **Portland**.
5. **Julio** spied a seaplane.
6. Another boy saw a **Flying Eagle**.
7. The plane was flying to **Canada**.
8. **Sarah** waved to the pilot.

Lesson 22, Action Verbs (P. 30)

Top:
1. chattered
2. drank
3. leaped
4. read
5. got

Middle:
1. search
2. grow
3. swing
4. buzz
5. roar

Bottom:
Sentences will vary.

Lesson 23, Verbs in the Present (P. 31)

Top:
1. rings
2. run
3. waves
4. talk
5. swings
6. makes
7. tells
8. plan

Bottom:
Sentences will vary.

Lesson 24, Verbs in the Past (P. 32)

Top:
1. like
2. P   turned
3. P   stopped
4. P   squeezed
5. pedal
6. P   rested

Bottom:
1. We entered the bike race.
2. We started the race together.
3. We walked our bikes up the hill.
4. The dogs chased our wheels.
5. I hoped to win.

Lesson 25, Linking Verbs (P. 33)

Top:
1. L
4. L
6. L
9. L
11. L

Bottom:
Sentences will vary.

Lesson 26, Using *Am, Is,* and *Are* (P. 34)

Line 1. are; is
Line 3. is
Line 4. am
Line 6. are; is
Line 8. am
Line 10. is
Line 12. am
Line 13. are
Line 14. are

Lesson 27, Using *Was* and *Were* (P. 35)

1. was
2. was
3. were
4. was
5. was
6. was
7. were
8. were
9. was
10. were
11. was
12. was
13. was
14. were

Lesson 28, Helping Verbs (P. 36)

Top:
Students should circle the words in bold.
1. The sun has **risen**.
2. The rooster had **remembered** to crow.
3. The cows have **chewed** their grass.
4. The girls had **collected** the eggs.
5. Dad has **baked** some fresh bread.
6. We have **eaten** breakfast.

Bottom:
1. I have walked to the park.
2. A gentle rain has started.
3. It had rained yesterday.
4. Pat had picked out an umbrella last week.

Lesson 29, Using Forms of *Do* and *See* (P. 37)

Top:
1. did
2. done
3. does
4. done
5. do
6. do

Bottom:
1. saw
2. see
3. saw
4. sees
5. see
6. seen

Lesson 30, Using Forms of *Give* and *Go* (P. 38)

Top:
1. give
2. gives
3. gave
4. given
5. given
6. gives
7. given
8. gave

Bottom:
1. go
2. goes
3. gone
4. goes

5. go
6. went
7. go
8. went

Lesson 31, Pronouns (P. 39)

Top:
1. She made popcorn for the class.
2. They love to eat popcorn.
3. Hot air tosses it around.
4. He put salt on his popcorn.
5. Don gave some popcorn to her.
6. Sue gave bowls to them.

Bottom:
Sentences will vary.

Lesson 32, Subject and Object Pronouns (P. 40)

Top:
1. O
2. S
3. S
4. O
5. S
6. O

Bottom:
1. We went to the rodeo.
2. The friendly cowgirl roped them.
3. He couldn't believe her strength.
4. The cowgirl gave us a smile when she won.

Lesson 33, Possessive Pronouns (P. 41)

Top:
1. their
2. My
3. Their
4. our
5. her
6. his

Bottom:
1. His
2. My
3. Her
4. Their
5. Our
6. Your
7. Its
8. His

Lesson 34, Using _I_ or _Me_ (P. 42)

1. Liz; I
2. her; me
3. Liz; me
4. Liz; I
5. Sally; I

6. Sally; I
7. Sally; me
8. Sally; I
9. Sally; me
10. Sally; I

Lesson 35, Adjectives (P. 43)

Top:
1. bright
2. noisy
3. great
4. old
5. Three
6. Funny

Bottom:
Sentences will vary.

Lesson 36, Comparing with Adjectives (P. 44)

Top:
1. longer
2. funniest
3. biggest
4. loudest
5. closest
6. higher

Bottom:
1. quicker
2. greatest
3. proudest
4. lighter
5. softer
6. older

Lesson 37, Using _A_ or _An_ (P. 45)

Top:
1. a
2. an
3. a
4. a
5. an
6. a
7. an
8. a
9. a
10. a
11. an
12. a
13. a
14. an
15. a
16. an
17. a
18. an
19. an
20. an

Bottom:
a cat
an ostrich
an owl

Lesson 38, Adverbs (P. 46)

Top:

HOW?	WHEN?	WHERE?
carefully	early	everywhere
happily	later	far
quickly	now	here
quietly	then	out

Bottom:
1. early   when
2. quietly   how
3. later   when
4. there   where

Lesson 39, Using *Good* and *Well* (P. 47)

Top:
1. good
2. well
3. good
4. well
5. good

Bottom:
Line 1.   good
Line 2.   well
Line 3.   good
Line 5.   good
Line 6.   well
Line 7.   good; good
Line 9.   well
Line 10.   good

Review (P. 48)

Students should circle the words in bold.
1. The garden will be full of **flowers**.
2. The **children** will mow the yard.
3. The **roses** are in the sun.
4. The **birds** love the birdbath.

1. **Greg** bought seeds at **Plant World**.
2. **Greg** scattered the seeds.
3. He waters his plants every **Monday**.
4. He'll have corn in **July**.

1. The daisies grow quickly.   present
2. The roses **were** droopy.   past
3. The pansies **are** colorful.   present

1. rests   4. see
2. am   5. does
3. was   6. go

1. has
2. has
3. have

Review (P. 49)

1. She
2. her
3. I
4. our
5. my
6. them

1. darkest
2. shorter
3. lowest
4. older
5. faster
6. greatest

1. quickly
2. softly
3. soon
4. brightly
5. early
6. very

1. well   4. well
2. good   5. good
3. well   6. good

Using What You've Learned (P. 50)

Monster Mack is looking at himself in the mirror. His hair looks like dry grass. It needs to be cut. His brown eyes flash and sparkle in the bright light. The smile on his face is like a half moon. It disappears when you see his nose. His nose is smaller than his ears. It is good that his ears are huge, though. They get everyone's attention when he wiggles them.

Using What You've Learned (P. 51)

Paragraphs will vary.

 Unit 4

Capitalization and Punctuation

Lesson 40, Capitalizing Days, Holidays, and Months (P. 52)

Top:
1. Mother's Day
2. winter
3. July
4. Saturday
5. June
6. spring
7. Thursday
8. April

Bottom:
1. This winter I am going to a parade on New Year's Day.
2. The parade is in January.
3. It is on Saturday.
4. Last summer I went to a parade on Labor Day.

Lesson 41, Capitalizing Names of People and Places (P. 53)

Top:
1. Uncle Brian
2. New York
3. Jamie Smith
4. my grandfather
5. Dallas
6. Florida
7. Aunt Sue
8. Charles
9. France
10. Montreal

Bottom:
1. We put on a play about Ramona Quimby.
2. Did your uncle from San Diego see it?
3. I think Aunt Sarah liked it.
4. Susan Allen had the part of Ramona.

Lesson 42, Beginning Sentences (P. 54)

1. Would you like to have a pony?
2. Elena has a pretty red pony.
3. Her pony's name is Rosie.
4. She rides her pony every day.
5. It is tiny, but fast.
6. The pony races through the fields.
7. Elena brushes her pony.
8. Then it takes a nap.
9. A pony is a fun pet.

Lesson 43, Ending Sentences (P. 55)

Top:
1. Guppies can live in a large bowl of water.
2. Does the water need to be cleaned?
3. Look at all the pretty colors!
4. Can you count how many there are?
5. What a long tail that guppy has!

Bottom:
1. Do you feed guppies dry food?
2. I can't believe how well they swim!
3. The biggest guppy is named Butch.
4. What is the little one's name?
5. I like him the best.

Lesson 44, Abbreviating Names of People and Places (P. 56)

Top:
1. Laura I. Wilder
2. Mrs. Tolan
3. Cherry Tree Rd.
4. Dr. Doolittle
5. A. A. Milne
6. Ms. T. Lowry
7. Quimby St.
8. Mrs. Banks
9. E. M. Thomas

Bottom:
Students should circle *Ms.* and *b.*
1. Ms.   2. B.

Lesson 45, Abbreviating Names of Days and Months (P. 57)

Top:
1. Thurs.   9. Oct.
2. Aug.   10. Sat.
3. Sun.   11. Dec.
4. Mar.   12. Wed.
5. Tues.   13. Nov.
6. Feb.   14. Fri.
7. Mon.   15. Jan.
8. Sept.   16. Apr.

Bottom:
Students should circle *sat, sept, fri,* and *oct.*
1. Sat.   Sept.
2. Fri.   Oct.

Lesson 46, Using Commas in Sentences (P. 58)

1. Yes, the band was in the parade.
2. Patty, Carlos, and Jo rode on a float.
3. We saw the bands, clowns, and floats.
4. Horses, fire engines, and flags came next.
5. No, I didn't stay until the end.
6. Yes, I wanted to stay.
7. We bought juice, nuts, and fruit to eat.
8. Yes, I waved to the woman on the horse.
9. No, she didn't see me.

Lesson 47, Writing Letters Correctly (P. 59)

Top:
Students should circle the words in bold.
1. New York, New York 10011
2. April 3, 1994
3. **dear gina,**
4. **your** friend,

Bottom:
1. May 7, 1994
2. Miami, Florida 33137
3. Dear Alicia,
4. With love,

Lesson 48, Using Apostrophes to Show Ownership (P. 60)

Top:
1. the pilot's hat
2. the woman's car
3. five dogs' bones
4. a kitten's toys
5. a clown's hat
6. many men's hats
7. the women's cars

8. a snowman's nose
9. ten kites' strings
10. the birds' nests

Bottom:
Sentences will vary.

Lesson 49, Using Apostrophes in Contractions (P. 61)

Top:
1. she's
2. we're
3. you'll
4. I've
5. he'd
6. she's

Middle:
1. hasn't
2. isn't
3. weren't
4. I'll
5. that's
6. wouldn't
7. they'll
8. there's

Bottom:
1. Jay hasn't seen the movie.
2. It's about a strange land.
3. One year winter doesn't come.
4. The people don't mind.

Lesson 50, Using Quotation Marks (P. 62)

1. "Yes, I will," said Carl. **or**
   Carl said, "Yes, I will."
2. "I want bread and butter," said Jane. **or**
   Jane said, "I want bread and butter."
3. "Butter feels soft," said Jane. **or**
   Jane said, "Butter feels soft."
4. "You have made a mess," said Carl. **or**
   Carl said, "You have made a mess."

Review (P. 63)

Students should circle the letters in bold.
1. **m**r. and **m**rs. **k**amp lived in a house on **m**ay **s**treet.
2. **o**ne **s**aturday the family cleaned the attic.
3. **e**llen found an old letter from **d**r. **r**. **m**. **w**ilson.
4. **t**he letter came all the way from **j**apan!
5. **w**e found a picture of roses, daisies, and tulips.
6. **d**id **d**ad take that photo on **v**alentine's **d**ay?
7. **n**o, my aunt took the photo last **a**pril.
8. **w**hat a mess the attic is!
9. **y**es, **m**om will clean out the attic next spring.
10. **e**llen, **j**ason, and **b**eth will help **m**om.

1. Tues.
2. Fri.
3. Mrs.
4. Elm St.

5. Dec.
6. M. C. Lee
7. Apr.
8. J. R. Adams
9. Feb.
10. Mon.
11. Smith Rd.
12. Mr.
13. Sat.
14. Dr. A. Roberts
15. Ms. N. Lincoln
16. Aug.

Review (P. 64)

Students should circle the letters in bold.
1. **b**irmingham, **a**labama 35205
2. **a**ugust 18, 1994
3. **d**ear **k**im,
4. **y**ours truly,
5. **d**ear **m**om,
6. **a**ustin, **t**exas 78759
7. **s**incerely,
8. **d**ear **d**r. **w**est,
9. **y**our friend,
10. **d**ec. 1, 1994
11. **g**lendora, **c**alifornia 91741
12. **w**ith love,

1. "This is Ellen's game," said Louisa.
2. Tom said, "It's her favorite."
3. "I'd like to play," said Mike.
4. Mike, Louisa, and Nancy sat down to play.
5. "It isn't hard to play," Tom said.
6. "Let's read the rules together," said Louisa.
7. "The game's rules are printed on the box," said Mike.
8. "We're ready to begin playing," said Louisa.
9. Mike said, "I'll go first."
10. "It's Nancy's turn to go first," said Louisa.
11. Nancy doesn't want to play.
12. She'd rather read Ellen's book.

Using What You've Learned (P. 65)

The underlined letters should be circled.

A Hidden Surprise

Jill's cat is named Sam. What a big, smart, beautiful cat he is! One summer day, Jill couldn't find him. Do you know where he was? He was under the porch with three new kittens. Jill said, "Your name is Samantha now."

Using What You've Learned (P. 66)

Letters will vary.

Unit 5 Composition

Lesson 51, Writing Sentences (P. 67)

Sentences will vary.

Lesson 52, Writing Paragraphs (P. 68)

Paragraphs will vary.

Lesson 53, Writing Topic Sentences (P. 69)

Students should underline the following sentences:

Many people are needed to put on a puppet show.

Shadow puppets are different from other kinds of puppets.

The person holding the puppet makes the puppet move.

Lesson 54, Writing Details (P. 70)

Students should circle the sentence in bold.

Our puppet show was a great success. Parents, friends, and neighbors came to see it. I am going to learn to swim this summer. Altogether, we sold twenty tickets and made $10.00. Rita already knows how to swim. Everyone liked the show and clapped for about two minutes after it was over. My uncle's name is Tony. He knows how to swim well. A good time was had by all!

Lesson 55, Arranging Details in Order (P. 71)

Top:
2
5
1
4
3

Bottom:
2
3
5
1
4

Lesson 56, Writing with Purpose (P. 72)

Sentences will vary.

Lesson 57, Choosing a Topic (P. 73)

Lists will vary.

Topics will vary.

Lesson 58, How-to Paragraph (P. 74)

Top:
It is not hard to make a soap-bottle king puppet.

Bottom:
Answers will vary.

Lesson 59, Writing a How-to Paragraph (P. 75)

Paragraphs will vary.

Lesson 60, Writing an Invitation (P. 76)

Invitations will vary.

Lesson 61, Writing a Telephone Message (P. 77)

Messages will vary.

Review (P. 78)

Top:
Sentences will vary.

Middle:
Students should circle the sentence in bold.

A break between acts in a play is needed. It allows time for the crowd to get up and stretch. Sarah is a very good math student. It lets the people in the show get ready for the rest of the play. It also gives time to prepare for the next act.

Bottom:
1. 3
   1
   4
   2
2. 3
   4
   1
   2

Review (P. 79)

Sentences will vary.

Invitations will vary.

Using What You've Learned (P. 80)

Messages will vary.

Using What You've Learned (P. 81)

Invitations will vary.

Paragraphs will vary.

 Unit 6 Study Skills

Lesson 62, Following Directions (P. 82)

1. south
2. Cook Street
3. west
4. Forest Road
5. 6

Lesson 63, Following Written Directions (P. 83)

1. a knife, popsicle sticks, a cookie sheet, a measuring cup, a tablespoon, a pot, waxed paper
2. bananas, chocolate chips, margarine
3. Push a popsicle stick into the center of each piece of banana.
4. Place the bananas in the freezer.

Lesson 64, Grouping (P. 84)

Top:

1. mouse	monkey	sheep	bird	
2. bread	egg	carrot	apple	fish
3. blue	red	purple	orange	
4. apple	orange	banana	grape	
5. pants	shirt	jacket	hat	
6. ball	circle	penny	orange	
7. bird	jet	rocket		
8. Peter	Mike	Josh	Tom	
9. Karen	Pam	Elaine	Melanie	
10. peas	carrots	beans	corn	
11. hammer	saw	shovel	rake	

Bottom:

Zoo Animals	Vegetables	Buildings
monkey	carrot	house
elephant	corn	school
lion	potato	store

Lesson 65, Using a Table of Contents (P. 85)

1. 6
2. Composition
3. 58
4. Sentences
5. 67
6. Review
7. Unit 3
8. 82
9. 8
10. 13
11. 96
12. 105
13. 14
14. Unit 1

Lesson 66, Using an Index (P. 86)

1. 108
2. 7, 11, 13, 97
3. 2, 10, 13, 96
4. 62, 64, 65, 103
5. no
6. 30, 48, 50, 51, 100
7. Multiple meanings
8. Students should list three of the following: commas, exclamation points, periods, question marks, quotation marks, apostrophes.
9. Writing process
10 77, 80, 105

Lesson 67, Alphabetical Order (P. 87)

1. canoe
2. oar
3. paddle

1. giant
2. glass
3. good

1. ranch
2. town
3. week

1. dream
2. east
3. soap

1. ball
2. beach
3. bounce

1. pole
2. price
3. pump

Lesson 68, Guide Words (P. 88)

Top:
1. add / chase
2. quack / weep
3. quack / weep
4. add / chase
5. quack / weep
6. add / chase
7. quack / weep
8. quack / weep

Bottom:
1. ill
2. arrow
3. dine
4. job
5. iron
6. weight
7. dad
8. ship
9. across
10. wonder
11. herd
12. post

Lesson 69, Dictionary: Definitions (P. 89)

1. carol
2. call
3. calf, carpet
4. carol
5. Sentences will vary.
6. Sentences will vary.
7. Sentences will vary.

Lesson 69, Dictionary: Definitions (P. 90)

1. 1
2. 1
3. 2
4. 2
5. 2
6. 3
7. 1
8. 2
9. 2
10. 1
11. 1
12. 2
13. 1
14. 1
15. 3
16. 2

Lesson 70, Dictionary: Pronunciation (P. 91)

Top:
1. pull
2. pierce
3. about, taken, pencil, lemon, circus

Bottom:
1. chose
2. letter
3. science
4. carton
5. these
6. measure
7. fuel

Review (P. 92)

1. a boat
2. Carefully open the shell by cracking it where the two halves join.
3. Cut a small sail from construction paper.

1. puppy, chick, kitten, lamb
2. fall, spring, summer, winter
3. apples, oranges, pears

1. clothes
2. meals
3. colors

Review (P. 93)

1. cage   **2.** bat   **3.** plow
   lake   bee   press
   seen   blue   puff

1. 46
2. 55, 63, 65, 66
3. 3, 4, 10, 12, 13, 96

1. to hunt
2. to be on one's feet
3. the stem of a plant
4. to put up with

1. awful
2. rhyme
3. van

Using What You've Learned (P. 94)

Fruits	Canned	Vegetables
bananas	canned soup	potatoes
apples		lettuce
		broccoli

Frozen	Meat
frozen orange juice	chicken
	hamburger
	bacon

1. Using What You've Learned
2. 33
3. 88
4. Using a Table of Contents
5. 13
6. Sentences

Using What You've Learned (P. 95)

Directions will vary.

Maps and directions will vary.

 # Final Reviews

Final Review, Unit 1 (P. 96)

1. S
2. A
3. A
4. A
5. A
6. A

1. to
2. too
3. two
4. there
5. hear
6. here

Final Review, Unit 1 (P. 97)

1. 2   **3.** 1
2. 1   **4.** 2

1. unable; not able
2. relive; live again
3. repay; pay again

1. worker; someone who works
2. dryer; something that dries
3. visitor; someone who visits

Students should circle the words in bold.
1. someone
2. **she's**
3. **I'll**
4. daylight

Final Review, Unit 2 (P. 98)

1. S
2. Q
3. E
4. C
5. X
6. Q
7. S
8. X
9. S
10. C

Students should circle the words in bold.
1. The new game **began**.
2. Jay **quickly bounced the ball**.
3. Vicki **picked up the pass**.
4. Todd **blocked the shot**.
5. Carl **jumped for the ball**.
6. The other team **got the ball**.

7. Lisa **tried to shoot a basket**.
8. The ball **bounced off the rim**.
9. Vicki **scored two points**.
10. Everyone **gave a loud cheer**.

1. happily
2. carefully
3. today
4. exactly
5. very, hard

Final Review, Unit 2 (P. 99)

1. Dan signaled to Jack and passed the ball.
2. Vincenté and Tamara wanted to play.
3. They won today but lost last week.

1. Mark enjoys all kinds of sports. His favorite sport is basketball.
2. Mark's mother used to play basketball. She was on a team in high school.
3. Mark finds a photo of his mother playing basketball. He shows it to his friend Tina.
4. Tina's mother is in the photo. Her mother used to play basketball, too.

Final Review, Unit 3 (P. 100)

1. P   inch
2. S   toes
3. S   buses
4. P   box
5. S   carts
6. P   tiger

1. C   (answers will vary)
2. P   state
3. C   (answers will vary)
4. P   lake

Students should circle the word in bold.
1. lives; present
2. visited; past
3. **was** past

1. saw
2. buy
3. runs
4. have
5. was
6. did

Final Review, Unit 3 (P. 101)

1. her
2. it
3. Her
4. her
5. I
6. us

1. largest
2. Some, green
3. Other, safer
4. Some, fresh
5. dangerous, other, these, hungry

Final Review, Unit 4 (P. 102)

1. December
2. winter
3. Monday
4. my sister
5. Louise
6. New Year's Day
7. California
8. Denver
9. Thanksgiving
10. Canada
11. Tomás
12. store

Students should circle the letters in bold.
1. **m**y family lives in **o**rlando, **f**lorida.
2. **i** go to school at **l**incoln **e**lementary.
3. **mrs. n. k**elly is my teacher this year.
4. **m**y class has been studying dinosaurs.
5. **s**he is taking us to a museum.
6. **w**e'll get to see dinosaur bones at the museum.
7. **t**he museum is north of our school.
8. **i**t is on **j**ones **s**treet near **a**cademy **t**heater.
9. **i**t is called the **c**harles **c. a**dler **m**useum.
10. **t**he museum is closed on **s**unday and **m**onday.
11. **w**e're going there on the first **t**uesday in **m**arch.
12. **mr. p**eterson, our principal, says we will have a great time.

Final Review, Unit 4 (P. 103)

1. Mrs. Kelly asked the people at the museum if they were ready for us.
2. Yes, they were ready for our class.
3. We saw dinosaur bones, snakes, and birds at the museum.
4. I didn't see all of the birds, but I saw all of the dinosaurs' bones.
5. We watched a film about baby dinosaurs.
6. Adam asked, "Have you ever seen a film about baby dinosaurs before?"
7. Hoan said, "No, I haven't."
8. "I liked the film, the cave, and the dinosaur footprints the best," said Neal.
9. "Let's plan another trip for next month," said Mrs. Kelly.
10. Do you think Mr. Peterson will let the class come back?

1. Dear Zach,
2. June 1, 1994
3. Houston, Texas 77072
4. Sincerely,
5. April 9, 1995
6. Your friend,
7. Dear Jesse,
8. Kansas City, Missouri 64114

Final Review, Unit 5 (P. 104)

Sentences will vary.

Students should circle the sentence in bold.

3 Next, practice saying your part in front of a mirror.
2 The first thing you can do to make yourself feel better is to get used to being on a stage. 4 Finally, ask some friends or family members if they will listen as you practice. 1 **Most people get scared when they must act in front of people.**

2 First, some students held imaginary cameras. 1 **Yesterday Ms. Yamata's class put on a television show.** _4 After the show was over, the class discussed what they had learned. 3 Then other students acted out a story._

Final Review, Unit 5 (P. 105)

Paragraphs will vary.

Messages will vary.

Final Review, Unit 6 (P. 106)

1. east
2. Oak Road
3. Town Hall

Breakfast	Dinner	Snacks
toast	fish	popcorn
pancakes	spaghetti	raisins

1. in the front of the book
2. It lists titles and page numbers of parts of the book.
3. in the back of the book
4. alphabetical order

Final Review, Unit 6 (P. 107)

1. rake
   sat
   scare
   leather / lie

2. cause
   cheer
   teeth

1. 1   2. 2

1. noisy
2. drawing
3. summer
4. fuss
5. aware
6. honor

 Tests

TEST: Unit 1, Pages 21–22, Teacher's Guide

1. D
2. B
3. A
4. D
5. A
6. C
7. B
8. D
9. B
10. C
11. D
12. A
13. C
14. B
15. B
16. A
17. C
18. B
19. D
20. A
21. D
22. B
23. C
24. A

TEST: Unit 2, Pages 23–24, Teacher's Guide

1. A
2. D
3. B
4. D
5. C
6. C
7. A
8. B
9. B
10. C
11. A
12. A
13. C
14. A
15. C
16. A
17. C

TEST: Unit 3, Pages 25–26, Teacher's Guide

1. B
2. B
3. D
4. A
5. C
6. D
7. B
8. C
9. B
10. A
11. C
12. C
13. A
14. D
15. A
16. D
17. C
18. D
19. B
20. B

21. D
22. A
23. C

3. A
4. D
5. B
6. B
7. B
8. D
9. D
10. A
11. B
12. D
13. C

TEST: Unit 4, Pages 27–28, Teacher's Guide

1. C
2. A
3. D
4. A
5. D
6. C
7. A
8. C
9. C
10. B
11. D
12. A
13. C
14. B
15. D
16. B
17. B
18. D
19. A
20. D

TEST: Unit 6, Pages 31–32, Teacher's Guide

1. C
2. D
3. B
4. A
5. B
6. D
7. B
8. B
9. B
10. A
11. C
12. D
13. C
14. B
15. A
16. C
17. D

TEST: Unit 5, Pages 29–30, Teacher's Guide

1. A
2. D

Choose the word pairs that are synonyms.

1. A ○ weep, cough   C ○ weep, link
   B ○ weep, sleep   D ○ weep, cry

2. A ○ pitch, run   C ○ pitch, ball
   B ○ pitch, throw   D ○ pitch, patch

3. A ○ shove, push   C ○ shove, play
   B ○ shove, hold   D ○ shove, take

4. A ○ funny, joke   C ○ funny, face
   B ○ funny, clown   D ○ funny, silly

Choose the word pairs that are antonyms.

5. A ○ on, off   C ○ on, top
   B ○ on, no   D ○ on, near

6. A ○ loud, lazy   C ○ loud, quiet
   B ○ loud, sound   D ○ loud, proud

7. A ○ heavy, thick   C ○ heavy, coat
   B ○ heavy, light   D ○ heavy, dark

8. A ○ before, ready   C ○ before, then
   B ○ before, early   D ○ before, after

Choose the homonym for each underlined word.

9. they're
   A ○ here   C ○ they are
   B ○ there   D ○ he is

10. too
    A ○ also   C ○ two
    B ○ from   D ○ three

11. hear
    A ○ ear   C ○ there
    B ○ listen   D ○ here

12. their
    A ○ they're   C ○ our
    B ○ his   D ○ here

13. here
    A ○ there   C ○ hear
    B ○ where   D ○ they are

14. to
    A ○ from   C ○ by
    B ○ too   D ○ toward

15. there
    A ○ place   C ○ here
    B ○ their   D ○ them

16. two
    A ○ to   C ○ three
    B ○ number   D ○ also

Name _____

Choose the correct meaning for each underlined word.

17. retell
    A ○ not telling
    B ○ say
    C ○ tell again
    D ○ untold

18. unlucky
    A ○ sad
    B ○ not lucky
    C ○ win
    D ○ lucky again

19. unhappy
    A ○ not sad
    B ○ happy again
    C ○ glad
    D ○ not happy

20. refill
    A ○ fill again
    B ○ not filled
    C ○ empty
    D ○ pour

Choose the correct meaning for the underlined word in each sentence.

21. I picked a date from the tree.
    A ○ when an event occurs
    B ○ find out how old something is
    C ○ an appointment
    D ○ a fruit

22. I brought a present to the party.
    A ○ happening now
    B ○ a gift
    C ○ to give something
    D ○ to be here

Choose the contraction.

23. A ○ her
    B ○ he
    C ○ he's
    D ○ his

Choose the compound word.

24. A ○ everyone
    B ○ wonderful
    C ○ each
    D ○ thing

Choose whether each sentence is a statement, a command, a question, or an exclamation.

1. The peaches taste very sweet.

   A ○ statement   **B** ○ question   **C** ○ command   **D** ○ exclamation

2. What a nice picture!

   A ○ statement   **B** ○ question   **C** ○ command   **D** ○ exclamation

3. Do you want to dance?

   A ○ statement   **B** ○ question   **C** ○ command   **D** ○ exclamation

4. I can't believe she won the prize!

   A ○ statement   **B** ○ question   **C** ○ command   **D** ○ exclamation

5. Take this to your teacher.

   A ○ statement   **B** ○ question   **C** ○ command   **D** ○ exclamation

Choose the sentence in which the subject is underlined and the predicate is circled.

6. A ○ The clown had (a monkey.)

   B ○ The clown (had a monkey.)

   C ○ The clown (had a monkey.)

7. A ○ Kate (rides that horse.)

   B ○ Kate rides (that horse.)

   C ○ Kate rides that (horse.)

8. A ○ His party was (fun.)

   B ○ His party (was fun.)

   C ○ His (party was fun.)

9. A ○ The pilot (shook our hands.)

   B ○ The pilot (shook our hands.)

   C ○ The (pilot shook our hands.)

10. A ○ My (birthday is next month.)

   B ○ My birthday is (next month.)

   C ○ My birthday (is next month.)

11. A ○ Anthony (plays the piano.)

   B ○ Anthony plays (the piano.)

   C ○ Anthony plays the (piano.)

Name _____

Choose the two sentences that can be combined to make the underlined sentence.

12. Kate and George played the tape.

   A ○ Kate played the tape.
      George played the tape.

   B ○ Kate played the tape.
      George played at home.

   C ○ Kate and George played.
      The tape played.

14. You can read, or we can talk.

   A ○ You can read.
      We can talk.

   B ○ You cannot read.
      We cannot talk.

   C ○ You and I can read.
      We can talk.

13. Corinne hopped and skipped.

   A ○ Corinne hopped.
      Corinne jumped.

   B ○ Corinne hopped.
      Sara skipped.

   C ○ Corinne hopped.
      Corinne skipped.

15. We can go, but we'll be late.

   A ○ We can't go.
      It's too late.

   B ○ We can go.
      We can stay.

   C ○ We can go.
      We'll be late.

Choose the two sentences that should replace the underlined sentence.

16. I like math and science, they are fun.

   A ○ I like math and science.
      They are fun.

   B ○ I like math and science they.
      Are fun.

   C ○ I like math.
      And science are fun.

17. The puppy is playful, it licks my face.

   A ○ The puppy is.
      Playful it licks my face.

   B ○ The puppy.
      Is playful it licks my face.

   C ○ The puppy is playful.
      It licks my face.

Choose the correct plural form of each underlined singular noun.

1. bat

   A ○ bates   **C** ○ batys

   B ○ bats   **D** ○ baties

3. lunch

   A ○ lunchs   **C** ○ lunchies

   B ○ lunchys   **D** ○ lunches

2. fox

   A ○ foxen   **C** ○ foxies

   B ○ foxes   **D** ○ foxs

4. dish

   A ○ dishes   **C** ○ dishies

   B ○ dishs   **D** ○ dishys

Choose the proper noun in each group of nouns.

5. A ○ boy   **B** ○ girl   **C** ○ José   **D** ○ man

6. A ○ land   **B** ○ fly   **C** ○ state   **D** ○ Canada

7. A ○ month   **B** ○ Friday   **C** ○ day   **D** ○ school

Choose the sentence that has a verb in the past.

8. A ○ She sees the president.

   B ○ She greets the president.

   C ○ She greeted the president.

   D ○ She is the president.

10. A ○ He was ready to go.

   B ○ He will be ready to go.

   C ○ He is ready to go.

   D ○ He goes.

9. A ○ They honk their horns.

   B ○ They honked their horns.

   C ○ They are noisy.

   D ○ A horn is noisy.

11. A ○ They see the movie.

   B ○ They are seeing the movie.

   C ○ They saw the movie.

   D ○ They will see the movie.

Name

Choose the correct word to complete each sentence.

12. The lion __ across the plain.

    A ○ runned   **B** ○ run   **C** ○ ran   **D** ○ running

13. The turtle moved __ .

    A ○ slowly   **B** ○ slow   **C** ○ slows   **D** ○ slowed

14. All the oranges __ gone.

    A ○ be   **B** ○ is   **C** ○ was   **D** ○ were

15. We had __ adventure.

    A ○ an   **B** ○ a   **C** ○ and   **D** ○ am

16. Give the plate to __ .

    A ○ our   **B** ○ I   **C** ○ they   **D** ○ him

17. Don't you feel __ ?

    A ○ a   **B** ○ an   **C** ○ well   **D** ○ good

18. I __ awake.

    A ○ is   **B** ○ were   **C** ○ are   **D** ○ am

19. Martin is the __ person I know.

    A ○ happier   **B** ○ happiest   **C** ○ happying   **D** ○ happy

20. Jenny and __ like to ride our bikes.

    A ○ she   **B** ○ I   **C** ○ me   **D** ○ them

21. Juan lives __ from school.

    A ○ new   **B** ○ good   **C** ○ early   **D** ○ far

22. What __ you need?

    A ○ do   **B** ○ does   **C** ○ done   **D** ○ doing

23. Doug is __ than Adam.

    A ○ tall   **B** ○ tallest   **C** ○ taller   **D** ○ talls

Choose the word or group of words that is written correctly.

1. **A** ○ monday   **C** ○ Tuesday   5. **A** ○ Paul bennett   **C** ○ paul Bennett

   B ○ april   **D** ○ december   **B** ○ paul bennett   **D** ○ Paul Bennett

2. **A** ○ winter   **C** ○ Summer   6. **A** ○ nov   **C** ○ Nov.

   B ○ Spring   **D** ○ january   **B** ○ Nov   **D** ○ nov.

3. **A** ○ labor day   **C** ○ labor Day   7. **A** ○ men's coats   **C** ○ mens' coats

   B ○ Labor day   **D** ○ Labor Day   **B** ○ mens coat's   **D** ○ mens coats

4. **A** ○ New York   **C** ○ New york   8. **A** ○ a dogs' bark   **C** ○ a dog's bark

   B ○ new York   **D** ○ new york   **B** ○ a dogs bark   **D** ○ a dogs's bark

Choose the sentence that is written correctly.

9. **A** ○ Carla lives on elm Street.   12. **A** ○ Let's go to the Bronx Zoo.

   B ○ carla lives on Elm street.   **B** ○ let's go to the bronx Zoo.

   C ○ Carla lives on Elm Street.   **C** ○ Let's go to the bronx Zoo.

   D ○ carla lives on elm Street.   **D** ○ let's go to the Bronx zoo.

10. **A** ○ mr. J. T. White left Sunday.   13. **A** ○ it's a beautiful day.

   B ○ Mr. J. T. White left Sunday.   **B** ○ it's a beautiful day!

   C ○ Mr. j. t. White left sunday.   **C** ○ It's a beautiful day.

   D ○ Mr. J T White left Sunday.   **D** ○ it's a beautiful day?

11. **A** ○ is the library open today?   14. **A** ○ Jim's brother will visit in march.

   B ○ is the Library open today?   **B** ○ Jim's brother will visit in March.

   C ○ Is the Library open today.   **C** ○ Jims brother will visit in March.

   D ○ Is the library open today?   **D** ○ jim's brother will visit in March.

Name _____   **27**

Choose the sentence that is written correctly.

15. A ○ The store sold fresh beans, carrots and peas

    B ○ The store sold fresh beans, carrots, and peas

    C ○ The store sold fresh beans carrots and peas.

    D ○ The store sold fresh beans, carrots, and peas.

16. A ○ I like to paint, said Rosa

    B ○ "I like to paint," said Rosa.

    C ○ I like to paint," said Rosa.

    D ○ I like to paint said Rosa.

17. A ○ No I can't play soccer.

    B ○ No, I can't play soccer.

    C ○ "No I can't play, soccer.

    D ○ No" I can't play soccer.

18. A ○ Wendy moved to Miami Florida.

    B ○ Wendy moved to "Miami" Florida.

    C ○ Wendy moved to, Miami Florida.

    D ○ Wendy moved to Miami, Florida.

19. A ○ Tom said, "I'll be home in an hour."

    B ○ Tom said, I'll be home in an hour.

    C ○ Tom said "I"ll be home in an hour.

    D ○ Tom said I'll be home in an hour.

20. A ○ Yes, I want to go, "said Carlos."

    B ○ "Yes I want to go" said Carlos

    C ○ Yes, I want to go, said Carlos.

    D ○ "Yes, I want to go," said Carlos.

Name _____

Read the paragraphs. Then choose the correct answer to each question.

A

Nathan is making a frozen treat. First, he makes a pitcher of juice. Next, he pours the juice into an ice cube tray. Nathan's sister is four years old. Then he freezes the juice. Finally, Nathan shares his frozen juice cubes with everyone.

B

Maria has a plan. First, she will cut her neighbor's grass. Maria had a birthday last week. Next, she will save her money. Then she will buy her mother a gift. Finally, Maria will give it to her.

1. What is the topic sentence in paragraph A?

   A ○ Nathan is making a frozen treat.

   B ○ First, he makes a pitcher of juice.

   C ○ Then he freezes the juice.

2. How many sentences do <u>not</u> give details in paragraph A?

   A ○ two   **C** ○ four

   B ○ three   **D** ○ one

3. What is the topic sentence in paragraph B?

   A ○ Maria has a plan.

   B ○ First, she will cut her neighbor's grass.

   C ○ Maria had a birthday last week.

4. How many sentences do <u>not</u> give details in paragraph B?

   A ○ two   **C** ○ four

   B ○ three   **D** ○ one

Choose the time order word from each sentence.

5. Then Nathan pours fruit juice.

   A ○ pours   **C** ○ fruit

   B ○ Then   **D** ○ Nathan

6. Finally, Nathan shares his cubes.

   A ○ Nathan   **C** ○ shares

   B ○ Finally   **D** ○ cubes

7. Next, Maria saved her money.

   A ○ saved   **C** ○ money

   B ○ Next   **D** ○ Maria

8. First, he makes juice.

   A ○ he   **C** ○ juice

   B ○ makes   **D** ○ First

Name _____   **29**

Choose the sentence that is written for the purpose described.

9. Which sentence tells how someone feels about walking to school?

    A ○ I walk two miles to get to school.

    B ○ I walk on a sidewalk to get to school.

    C ○ I get to school by riding my bicycle.

    D ○ Walking to school is an exciting way to begin the day.

10. Which sentence might be in a make-believe story about a horse?

    A ○ The horse spread its wings and flew across the cloudless sky.

    B ○ I let the horse graze in the field.

    C ○ Akiko would like to learn how to take care of a horse.

    D ○ The horse was brown and had a black mane and tail.

11. Which sentence describes a real hospital?

    A ○ The hospital was built on Pluto, a planet far from Earth.

    B ○ The hospital was made up of four white brick buildings.

    C ○ Doctors like to work in hospitals.

    D ○ We have a hospital in our town.

Choose the correct answer to each question.

12. Which of the following is not important when taking a telephone message?

    A ○ the name of the person calling

    B ○ the phone number of the person calling

    C ○ the date and time of the call

    D ○ the age of the person calling

13. Which of the following is not important when writing an invitation?

    A ○ who   **C** ○ how

    B ○ when   **D** ○ where

© 1995 Steck-Vaughn Company.

Name _____

Choose the group of words that belongs with the underlined word.

1. <u>toys</u>

   A ○ balls, circles, dimes

   B ○ dolls, puppets, brothers

   C ○ puzzles, dolls, balls

   D ○ bikes, wagons, fences

2. <u>fruit</u>

   A ○ apple, red, seed

   B ○ orange, milk, toast

   C ○ plum, peach, purple

   D ○ pear, orange, apple

3. <u>clothing</u>

   A ○ button, neck, shirt

   B ○ socks, skirt, pants

   C ○ gloves, hands, scarf

   D ○ belt, back, leather

4. <u>pets</u>

   A ○ dogs, cats, birds

   B ○ bears, dogs, bark

   C ○ bees, flowers, honey

   D ○ lions, mane, tail

Choose the group of words that does <u>not</u> describe a table of contents.

5. **A** ○ lists titles of units or chapters

   B ○ lists entries in alphabetical order

   C ○ is in the front of a book

   D ○ lists page numbers

Choose the group of words that does <u>not</u> describe an index.

6. **A** ○ lists page numbers

   B ○ lists entries in alphabetical order

   C ○ lists subjects

   D ○ lists titles of units or chapters

Name _____

Choose the group of words that is in alphabetical order.

7. **A** ○ cover   **B** ○ cover   **C** ○ fair
     cloth   cream   block
     desk   crown   chin
     high   head   hook

8. **A** ○ son   **B** ○ spend   **C** ○ tall
     snow   star   test
     story   street   stone
     stand   sweet   stand

Choose the word that would be on the same page as the underlined guide words.

9. <u>brick</u> / <u>clear</u>   **A** ○ box   **B** ○ care   **C** ○ bed   **D** ○ cup

10. <u>send</u> / <u>those</u>   **A** ○ sound   **B** ○ same   **C** ○ turn   **D** ○ two

11. <u>mix</u> / <u>mountain</u>   **A** ○ myth   **B** ○ next   **C** ○ moist   **D** ○ leave

12. <u>teeth</u> / <u>terrible</u>   **A** ○ toast   **B** ○ table   **C** ○ trouble   **D** ○ tender

Choose the sentence that goes with definition number 1.

13. **A** ○ Put butter on the roll.

    B ○ The roll is very brown.

    C ○ Did the dog roll over?

    D ○ Save the roll for me.

> **roll 1.** To move by turning over and over. **2.** A kind of bread or cake.

Choose the word that matches the respelling.

14. (fîers)   **A** ○ fires   **B** ○ fierce   **C** ○ furs   **D** ○ fears

15. (wind)   **A** ○ wind   **B** ○ windy   **C** ○ wide   **D** ○ went

16. (hwut)   **A** ○ wait   **B** ○ wheat   **C** ○ what   **D** ○ hut

17. (fīt)   **A** ○ fit   **B** ○ fifth   **C** ○ feet   **D** ○ fight

> at; āpe; fär; câre; end; mē; it; īce; pîerce; hot; ōld, sông; fôrk; oil; out; up; ūse; rüle; pu̇ll; tûrn; chin; sing; shop; thin; this; hw in white; zh in treasure. The symbol ə stands for the unstressed vowel sound in about, taken, pencil, lemon, and circus.